Original title:
Potted Possibilities

Copyright © 2025 Creative Arts Management OÜ
All rights reserved.

Author: Giselle Montgomery
ISBN HARDBACK: 978-1-80581-887-8
ISBN PAPERBACK: 978-1-80581-414-6
ISBN EBOOK: 978-1-80581-887-8

Aromatic Adventures

In a kitchen, herbs do dance,
Basil twirls in airy prance.
Oregano sings a fragrant tune,
While thyme plots to charm the moon.

Mint tells jokes, they're quite a hoot,
Chives wear hats that are so cute.
Parsley attempts a stand-up show,
But keeps forgetting where to go.

Exploring the Green Terrain

A cactus dreams of sandy shores,
While climbing vines chart out their tours.
Pansies ponder life's grand scheme,
As sunflowers bask in sunbeam dreams.

Lettuce plays hide and seek with light,
Radishes giggle in pure delight.
In this patchwork of shy delights,
Even weeds throw wild, fun-filled fights.

Parable of the Pots

A pot once dreamed of holding gold,
But now it's just a tale retold.
With soil and seeds, it found its bliss,
In growing talent none could miss.

The comical chives grew long and lean,
While potatoes plotted to be seen.
Smiling daisies, hats in hand,
Stood tall, in this quiet land.

Growth Beyond the Garden

A sprout declared, 'I'll reach the sky!'
While beans laughed, "You cannot fly!"
Yet in this amusing little turf,
Each tried to prove their little worth.

The flowers jested, 'Who'll take the lead?'
As they danced to nature's own creed.
With bugs as jesters in the scene,
Together, they formed a merry team.

A Symphony of Sprouts

Tiny leaves dance in a jar,
Singing songs of 'look, how bizarre!'
With roots that twist and stalks that sway,
They're plotting a party for garden play.

A carrot in a cap, what a sight!
Radishes drumming, feeling quite bright.
Tomatoes wear shades, soaking up sun,
While peas in a pod just want to run!

Nurtured by Nature

The soil's a party, oh what a thrill,
Each seed is a joker, ready to spill.
With petals like confetti, they bloom and burst,
A garden glee, oh how they thirst!

Butterflies are bouncers, keeping the peace,
While worms do the limbo, never cease.
Daisies wear glasses, thinking they're cool,
In this nutty patch, nature's the fool!

Vessel of Green Dreams

Inside a pot, dreams take flight,
Herbs whisper secrets, sharing delight.
Basil's got jokes, parsley is coy,
Mint crackles laughter, oh what joy!

A rogue cactus vows to breakdance too,
While chives recite poetry, just a few.
In this vessel, fun never ends,
Each sprout is a buddy, each leaf a friend!

Whimsy in the Windowsill

On the sill, a mishmash of green,
Chives act like divas, never serene.
A fern's got a flick, waving hello,
While succulents pose for a glam photo!

Spices gossip about yesterday's rain,
And basil's convinced he's king of the lane.
With sunlight and laughter, all things align,
This merry band grows, sip tea and dine!

Vines of Connection

In a pot, they twist and twine,
Greens entwined, both yours and mine.
Laughter bounces, roots get snug,
What a mess, a loving hug!

Oh, the thrill of sharing soil,
With my neighbor's plans, I toil.
But whose tomato wins the race?
Guess we'll just have to embrace!

Reaching for the Sky

Little sprouts with dreams so high,
Stretching leaves, they do comply.
Sunshine whispers, 'give it a go!'
Up they climb, a leafy show!

Each small pot, a lofty dream,
Yet they giggle, unable to scheme.
'Okay, right! No more water fun!'
Watch them dance in morning sun!

The Art of Fertility

Gardening tips from a wise old gnome,
He says, 'Give love, make it home!'
Fertilizer? Might need a hug,
Or is it time to just chug-a-lug?

Seeds in circles, what a swirl,
Who knew dirt could make you twirl?
Thumps and bumps, it's quite absurd,
Playing tag with each loose herd!

Unfolding the Future

Tiny leaves push through the dirt,
What's emerging? A shy dessert!
Cactus jokes and ferny puns,
The garden laughs, it's far from done!

Butterfly dreams and wormy grins,
This growth game? Everyone wins!
Wait and see, it's all a jest,
In the end, we'll all be blessed!

Nature's Blueprint

In a pot, a tiny seed,
A dream of growth, indeed!
It winks with leafy cheer,
No need for soil to steer.

A cactus dreams of rain,
While succulents dance in vain,
The soil just rolls its eyes,
As plants plot their surprise.

The herbs hold wild debates,
About their spicy fates,
While worms write secret notes,
In their underground boats.

With every sunbeam caught,
Their plans begin to knot,
A garden's joyful scheme,
Life's most ridiculous dream.

Serendipitous Seeds

Once sprouted on a whim,
A daisy's chance to swim,
It twirls in summer's light,
And laughs at worms in fright.

A mushroom thinks it's bold,
In a pot of marigold,
"Why can't I reach the stars?"
Says it with flowery bars.

The beans hold a parade,
In shades that never fade,
While their roots play tag,
With every leg and wag.

A rogue potato's tale,
Unfolds upon the trail,
It wears a tiny hat,
And laughs with every chat.

Nurturing New Horizons

In a bowl with a bizarre twist,
A fern dreams of a mist,
While pots jostle around,
To find some joyful ground.

The pepper plant throws shade,
Its spicy jokes well-made,
Chili peppers, in a line,
Red like a crafty sign.

A basil sprout stands tall,
Taking charge, it calls all,
"Join me on this quest,
To season life's best fest!"

With laughter in the air,
Tending plants everywhere,
A garden gathered close,
In this odd little host.

A Tapestry of Green

Amongst the leaf-clad friends,
A chorus that transcends,
The ferns tell silly tales,
Of minty shipwrecked sails.

They sport their leafy hats,
While plotting pranks with rats,
Sunshine aims to conspire,
With a blast of warm desire.

The thyme gets caught in knots,
Amid a sea of pots,
With every twist, it sways,
In whimsical displays.

A jolly little crew,
In every shade of hue,
Together they shall grow,
In laughter's lovely flow.

Tendrils of Hope

In a pot, a sprout peeks out,
With dreams of growing stout.
It wiggles in a playful dance,
Hoping for a sunlit chance.

Tiny leaves, a twisting fate,
Questioning if it's too late.
Watered with laughter every day,
It tries to chase the clouds away.

Garden Guardians

A gnome stands guard, with a grin,
  Watching herbs become a win.
He whispers to the creeping thyme,
'Let's make this garden truly prime!'

The trowel chuckles in the dirt,
  'Plant a seed, you'll feel the flirt!'
With potting soil and lots of cheer,
  Together they grow year after year.

Potent Roots of Change

From a seed, a sprout will rise,
With leaves that dare to reach the skies.
Beneath the surface, roots will crawl,
Creating chaos, having a ball.

They switch places with worms so sly,
'The ground is ours, let's give it a try!'
In soil's embrace, they wiggle and twist,
Crafting a mess, but who can resist?

The Beauty Within the Bound

In a crowded pot, they jostle and fight,
Each trying hard to steal the light.
A daisy dreams of worlds afar,
While a cactus brags, 'I'm the star!'

Mismatched friends, a quirky bunch,
They laugh and swap soil during lunch.
With everyday antics, they thrive,
Reminding us to just feel alive!

The Secret Life of Soil

In the dark, the worms do wiggle,
Where roots and secrets softly giggle.
The plants conspire with dirt so bold,
In whispers shared, their tales unfold.

Mushrooms wear hats, so very chic,
While beetles join in, with a tiny tweak.
Caterpillars don their finest shoes,
In the soil's rave, who can refuse?

Ants march forward, a busy parade,
Trading secrets in the dirt brigade.
Rain drops sprinkle like confetti bright,
In this underground, a party's alight!

Transformations in Terracotta

Once a lump of clay, oh so plain,
Now a vessel for dreams, it's no disdain.
With pots that giggle when filled with cheer,
Planting tales of growth, loud and clear.

Cacti wear crowns, poking fun with glee,
While ferns giggle softly, 'Look at me!'.
A sunflower sways, not one bit shy,
"I'm the king here, just wait for the sky!"

Every pot holds a surprise inside,
With roots like dancers, twirling wide.
The soil sings songs, in rhythmic flow,
While flowers whisper secrets, 'You should know.'

Windowsill Wisdom

On the edge of the world, a small plant shines,
Sipping sunlight, ignoring all signs.
It wisecracks daily, "Look at me go!
The sun's my DJ, I'm stealing the show!"

Dust bunnies laugh, as they gather near,
"Is that parsley on the menu, dear?"
Silly herbs in a dance so spry,
Chasing shadows that flutter by.

Tomatoes flirt with a drape of lace,
While busy bees buzz, just in case.
Windowsill tales bring giggles and light,
Together we grow, from morning to night.

Delicate Dances of Nature

Petals spin like a ballerina's twirl,
As bees take cues, in a buzzing whirl.
Ladybugs join in with a shiny flair,
Dancing soft steps in the fragrant air.

The breeze plays music, a light-hearted tease,
Fluttering leaves catch the rhythm with ease.
Each bloom throws a party, in colors so bright,
Nature's own gala, a marvelous sight!

From raindrops to sunshine, they prance and sway,
Every bug and bloom has a part to play.
Nature's a stage with a lively cast,
In this grand ballet, we're all here at last!

Cultivated Wishes

In a pot sat a chive, so brave,
Dreaming of being a gourmet wave.
It yelled out loud, 'Give me a chef!'
While the basil laughed, 'You'll starve to death!'

A tomato claimed its royal bluff,
Said, 'I'm a fruit, we're not that tough!'
The garlic just rolled its eyes and stank,
'We all know it's pasta that gets the rank.'

Kitchen Counter Cornucopia

On the counter, a pumpkin felt grand,
Wearing a hat, it thought it could stand.
But when the carrot called out for a dance,
The pumpkin tripped, it had no chance!

A teapot laughed, water shook with glee,
'This kitchen's a circus, just wait and see!'
The herbs started chirping like birds on a spree,
Each one with a dream of their own recipe!

Journey of the Seed

A tiny seed, full of dreams and pride,
Hitchhiked a ride on a gardener's slide.
'What do you do when you leave the shell?'
It wondered aloud, 'Will it be swell?'

The soil just chuckled, 'You'll soon find out!'
'Just stretch your roots, dance with no doubt!'
And there it went, through dirt and grime,
Rising to the sun, what a ride in time!

Petals of Possibility

In the sunshine, flowers found their cheer,
With petals that whispered, 'We're almost here!'
The dandelion, with dreams of flight,
Floated away, much to everyone's fright!

A daisy said, 'Let's start a show!'
With butterflies fluttering, all in a row.
Each petal giggled, dreaming of fame,
'Who knew growing up could be such a game?'

Sprouts of Ambition

In a pot by the window, a dream starts to sprout,
Sunshine and water, and that's what it's about.
Seeds of great ideas, like green little beans,
Wiggle and giggle, on their tiny machines.

A radish with swagger, a carrot with flair,
Telling their stories, without any care.
They plot and they plan, in their cozy little space,
Chasing the daydreams at a very quick pace.

Herbs with their hats, all ready to clash,
Sassy little sprouts, having a grand bash.
With thyme on their side, they dance in a line,
Each leaf with a laugh, oh how they do shine!

What fun in the dirt, where dreams take their flight,
Digging for glory, under soft moonlight.
Who knew that a pot could contain such a scene?
A riot of growth, in a world so serene!

The Oasis in a Tile

On a bathroom wall, where dreams sprout and grow,
A cactus is thinking, 'I'm the star of the show!'
Bathroom bringers of joy, in colors so bright,
They stand tall and proud, all ready for flight.

A fern whispers secrets, while resting in peace,
In this crazy domain, they find their release.
With bubbles and giggles, they fill every space,
In this tiled oasis, they each find their place.

A succulent greets you, when you step in the room,
Wearing a grin, it chases away gloom.
With a wink from the plant, troubles drift away,
In this lush little haven, all worries will sway.

With water and sunlight, they dance without care,
Creating their magic, spreading laughter in air.
In pots and in tiles, dreams bloom side by side,
An oasis of happiness, where joy takes pride!

Snippets of Nature's Resolve

In a patch on the porch, little sprouts play a game,
Tiny green warriors, they're making their claim.
With dirt on their boots, they stand oh so tall,
Declaring their triumph, no pot is too small.

A mint with a grin, flavoring the air,
While daisies in helmets brave the sunny glare.
They form little squads, with smiles they combine,
Nature's small battalion, in their leafy design.

Against all odd weeds, they stand by their roots,
Gathering courage in their leafy green suits.
With bullfrogs as cheerleaders, they hop with delight,
Promising laughter, fighting wrongs with the right.

When rain clouds approach, they won't run away,
In each drop, they find fortune, come what may.
With grit and with giggles, they spread all around,
Snippets of nature, where joy can be found!

Budding Futures

In the garden of dreams, where the fruits want to play,
Budding little wonders, brightening the day.
Tomatoes with plans, peppers on the rise,
Each budding future, a fun surprise!

A pumpkin in sneakers, ready to roll,
With visions of glory, reaching for gold.
Together they laugh, like no dream's too wide,
A veggie convention, with pride as their guide.

Cabbages chime in, with a raucous cheer,
'We're destined for coleslaw, oh have no fear!'
Carrots in the back, with tales from the ground,
Whispering sweet secrets, all around sound.

As they grow in their pots, they spread lots of cheer,
Budding futures with laughter, a party so near.
So here's to the journey, where dreams intertwine,
In the laughter of foliage, all futures align!

Sprouts of Intention

A seed once dropped in a pot,
Said, "Grow tall, or not!"
With sunshine up above,
And hopes filled with love.

The sprout looked up with glee,
"Look at me, can't you see?"
I'll dance with every breeze,
Until I'm big as trees!

The neighbors all would stare,
As I sprouted everywhere.
"Just give me room to shine!
I swear I'll feel divine!"

In this little patch of earth,
I'll show you what I'm worth.
A forest in a cup,
So watch me, don't give up!

Greenhouse of Hope

In a glass house so grand,
Plants of all forms take a stand.
They laugh and joke all day,
In their leafy cabaret.

One cucumber said with pride,
"Watch me roll, I'm bona fide!"
While tomatoes strut around,
In this garden party found.

The air is filled with cheer,
As flowers bloom year by year.
"With watering cans, we'll sing,
As sunshine's our king!"

In this greenhouse of dreams,
Life is more fun than it seems.
With laughter as our companion,
We'll grow like plants in a canyon!

Soil and Serenity

In the soil, I dig a hole,
Searching for my garden soul.
Earthworms wiggle, dirt flies high,
"I'm the king!" they seem to cry.

"Hey there, little sprout!" I shout,
"What if I eat you out?"
"Not a chance!" it giggles back,
"I'm growing roots, that's the knack!"

A rock looked on with a frown,
"Why cannot I sprout a crown?"
"You just need a little break,
And a sunny side to make!"

In this patch of vibrant ground,
Where silly truths abound.
Together we will thrive,
In this quirky, lively hive!

Cultivating Kindness

With a tiny shovel in hand,
I'm off to make a band.
Plants grow tall with happy tunes,
Spreading joy beneath the moons.

A daisy with a flair,
Said, "Come see my lovely hair!"
While daisies danced in a line,
"Kindness blooms, isn't it fine?"

Neglect not the humble weeds,
They too have growing needs.
"Let's share the sun and the rain,
Together, we'll bloom again!"

In a garden full of cheer,
We cultivate without fear.
We plant a seed, we shall find,
In every blossom, kindness entwined!

Colors of Growth

In a pot so small and round,
Grow a rainbow from the ground.
Red and yellow, blue and green,
A garden party, quite the scene!

With tiny sprouts that jiggle and sway,
They catch the light in a playful way.
Crayons in dirt, a painter's delight,
Nature's canvas, bold and bright!

Each blossom has a silly grin,
Just waiting for the fun to begin.
They tell jokes in the morning sun,
These leafy friends, oh, what a run!

So let your imagination flow,
In this quirky green tableau.
With every bloom, a giggle grows,
In this pot of joy, anything goes!

Whispering Leaves

Leaves are gossiping, oh so sly,
Telling tales of the sky.
'Heard a rumor, got a tip,
That worms are planning a dance trip!'

They flutter softly in the breeze,
Swapping secrets with such ease.
A leafy choir in vibrant hues,
Performing songs of morning dues.

In the afternoon, they shade and play,
Making shadows come out to stay.
With every rustle, laughter spills,
These green comedians bring such thrills!

So join the party beneath the sun,
Where leaves, like friends, all have their fun.
Listen close to their merry schemes,
In this garden, we float on dreams!

Hands in the Earth

Digging deep with hands so small,
Finding treasures beneath it all.
Worms wiggling, dirt flying high,
'Hey, that's my lunch!' a beetle will cry!

Fingernails coated, quite a sight,
Guess it's time for a garden fight!
Who can plant the silliest seed?
The sprout takes lead, that's the greed!

The tulips peek with cheeky flair,
'Look at us! We haven't a care!'
Hands in dirt, the fun's alive,
In this muck, we surely thrive!

So turn the soil, make it dance,
Each seed's hoping for a chance.
With laughter and soil on our sleeves,
We're planting dreams with giggly leaves!

Floating on Green Dreams

On a leaf boat, we sail away,
Drifting slowly through the day.
With petals as sails, we glide and twirl,
In a world where giggles swirl.

Toss the weeds, they start to pout,
'We want in!' they uselessly shout.
But we're off on a frolicking spree,
Seeking sunshine and a bumblebee!

Each flower waves as we float by,
Chasing butterflies that flit and fly.
They laugh at us, laughing loud,
In this green sea, we feel so proud!

So come along, dear friend of mine,
Let's ride this wave of joy divine.
With every dip, a chuckle streams,
In this vessel of our green dreams!

Overgrown Aspirations

In a garden where dreams spill and stray,
A carrot debates joining a ballet.
Tomatoes roll in laughter so loud,
While radishes blush, feeling quite proud.

A sunflower sways, wearing shades of green,
Whispers of grandeur, a grander scene.
But weeds crash the party, uninvited,
With hopes of becoming the most excited.

The peas throw confetti, a veggie parade,
While lettuce is lounging, totally unmade.
Dirt on their faces, they giggle and hop,
In their overgrown world, they never will stop.

Blooms of Potential

In a pot on the shelf, a cactus dreams big,
Planning a dance with a brightly green fig.
Succulents gossip about the great heights,
While dandelions practice their wild, grassy flights.

Pansies in purple, and daisies in white,
Complain about pests who nibble all night.
But they laugh as they plot their flowered escape,
In this world of their dreams, they can never break shape.

With petals like feathers, they challenge the air,
Hoping to show that they're bright and quite rare.
In this tiny pot, where dreams take a swing,
Every bloom has a tale, they've plenty to bring.

Roots of Reflection

Buried beneath, the roots hold a song,
Each twist and turn, where they feel they belong.
With whispers of secrets, they tug at the soil,
In their underground world, they endlessly toil.

They ponder the sun, and the joy of the rain,
While pulling each other through the joys and the pain.
With tangled connections, they giggle and sway,
Plotting their paths for a better today.

Shy bulbs make plans for a festival bright,
Hoping the garden will join in the light.
"Let's break the surface, let's dance on the grass!
And maybe together, we'll explore, and we'll pass!"

Tiny Terracotta Hopes

In terracotta homes, dreams take their seats,
Giggling with glee as they hum little beats.
Each sprout holds a secret, each leaf tells a lie,
With wishes for sunbeams that reach for the sky.

Little pots whisper of trips to the wind,
Delighted by stories of places they've pinned.
With soil as their stage, they twirl and they shine,
Finding that happiness can glow from a vine.

A thimble of water, a sprinkle of cheer,
These tiny ambitions have nothing to fear.
As they grow into laughter, in playful displays,
With tiny terracotta hopes, they spend their days.

The Hidden Life Underground

Beneath the soil, where secrets hide,
Tiny critters throw a garden pride.
Worms dance and twirl in a sandy spree,
While roots gossip, 'O, what will be?'

Mice plot mischief, they nibble away,
While beetles argue, 'It's my turn to play!'
Under the surface, a raucous band,
Their concert loud, it's rather grand.

Ants march in line, a disciplined crew,
Hauling tiny treasures, 'Look what we grew!'
In this wild world, they laugh and thrive,
Who knew such fun could be alive?

So when you look down, don't just see dirt,
A riot of life, in fun they flirt.
Under your feet, a carnival reigns,
Where laughter sprouts amidst tangled veins.

Cultivating a Vision

With dreams in hand, I grab a pot,
Imagining flowers in a colorful lot.
Seeds are stacked high, a wobbly tower,
As I contemplate their coming power.

Dirt flies everywhere, what a mess!
I hope these seeds don't second guess.
A sprinkle of water, a dash of glee,
'Grow fast, my friend, or else I'll flee!'

The label says 'bloom,' but they look like grass,
Did I read it wrong, or is it just sass?
With every sprout, there's magic to share,
Fun surprises lurking beneath my care.

So here's to the journey, let's not be shy,
Together we'll grow, you and I.
In pots we trust, with laughter and cheer,
Let's cultivate visions, year after year!

Enchanted Growth

Once a tiny seed was snuggled tight,
In a cozy pot, it dreamt of flight.
Whispers of sunlight and breezy chats,
Promised a banquet of chittering sprats.

Leaves yawned wide, like sleepy folks,
Stretching and dancing among the blokes.
'Hey, I can see, I'm no longer shy!'
Said the timid sprout, reaching for the sky.

Friends came along, each quirky in style,
A cactus with humor that made us smile.
Butterflies fluttered, not paying the rent,
Joining the party, so cheeky and bent.

With every inch gained, a tangle of fun,
Laughter erupted, the journey begun.
In this garden of whimsy, oh what a sight,
Where growth is enchanted, and everything's right.

Leaves of Destiny

Three little leaves, oh what a crew!
They giggle and shimmer in the morning dew.
Bright sunshine makes them dance in glee,
'What will we be? Oh, can you see?'

'Let's become a hat or a fan, why not?
We'll cause such a stir, now give it a shot!'
They spin and twist in the warm, soft breeze,
Creating a ruckus among the trees.

The squirrels look on, with chuckles to spare,
As the leaves plot mischief in midair.
'Watch us float down, straight into your snack,
You never know, we might just come back!'

So here's to the leaves, on a whimsy quest,
Painting the world with fun, at its best.
In nature's theater, where all can see,
Destiny plays out, with a leaf's jubilee!

From Dirt to Delight

In the mud where plants reside,
Worms wiggle, trying to hide.
A tiny seed, with dreams so grand,
Hopes to sprout and take a stand.

Water spills in joyful streams,
Plants are dancing, it seems!
A little sun and chirp from birds,
Life is more than just the words.

With every sprout, there's laughter near,
Who knew dirt could bring such cheer?
Tiny leaves peek with a grin,
In the garden, fun begins!

So here's to plants, our silly pals,
Growing along with snorting gals.
From roots to stems, they shout hooray,
Dirt and glee come out to play!

Canvas of Growth

On my porch, a pot so bright,
Splashes of colors, what a sight!
A flower's face, a wink, a smile,
Growing taller by the while.

Brushes made of leaves and sun,
Painting greens, oh what fun!
Each petal's hue, a wild surprise,
Nature's art, with open skies.

With raindrops like tiny pearls,
It twirls and sways, oh how it twirls!
Insects join the funky beat,
Buzzy friends, oh what a treat!

Every day brings joys anew,
A canvas colored just for you.
Mixing laughter like palette paint,
Each bloom a story from a saint!

Garden of Dreams

In a garden, dreams take flight,
Tomatoes sing with all their might.
The carrots giggle underground,
In this plot, joy's always found.

Bumblebees buzz a silly tune,
Underneath the cheerful moon.
With daisies dancing, having fun,
Dreams and laughter on the run.

Every sprout has tales to share,
Of squirrel chases in the air.
Fables woven through each vine,
In this garden, all is fine!

So, if you wish for joy's embrace,
Come take a stroll, find your place.
In the garden of sweet smiles,
Dreams are growing, stretching miles!

Seeds of Tomorrow

Little seeds, oh what a tease,
Hide inside those cozy trees.
With a wink and playful laugh,
Ready to carve their own path.

They plot and plan beneath the ground,
Hatching dreams without a sound.
With each new sprout, they burst with zeal,
Nature's jesters, oh so real!

On a rainy day, they sip and play,
Making mud pies all the way.
A cabbage ball, a sunflower's game,
Each one's dancing, wild and tame!

So when you plant, don't hold back,
Join the seeds on this fun track.
Tomorrow's blooms, a joyful cheer,
In this garden, smiles appear!

Tales from the Terracotta

In a pot sat a tiny sprout,
It whispered tales without a doubt.
"I dream of heights, I'll be a tree,"
A clever plan for all to see.

A snail rolled up, said, "Not so fast!"
"A tree needs time, it's built to last."
"But I can climb!" the sprout replied,
"With every inch, my dreams abide!"

A ladybug soon joined the chat,
"Let's grow a house, a little flat!"
To fix it up with colors bright,
With tiny windows, what a sight!

In terracotta, dreams collide,
With soil so rich, they can't abide.
They laugh and dance beneath the sun,
In every pot, there's room for fun!

Shaping Tomorrow's Garden

The seeds conspired in a row,
"Let's make a garden, steal the show!"
A carrot popped up with a grin,
"A tasty prize, let's begin!"

Tomato said, "I'll wear a crown!"
"And I'll grow tall, I won't back down!"
Each sprout had dreams of grandeur here,
With plans to make the neighbors leer.

The radish teased, "I'll dig so deep,"
"You'll never catch me, not a peep!"
With roots that stretch beneath the ground,
They schemed and plotted all around.

In shadows their jests began to sprout,
With laughter echoing all about.
They shaped a garden, bold and bright,
Tomorrow's blooms are quite the sight!

Oasis of Edible Dreams

In pots of clay, a feast was born,
Where every herb had dreams to scorn.
"I'll be a pesto, rich and green!"
A basil's goal was quite the scene.

Mint chimed in, "I'll be a brew,
Refreshing tales that grow anew!"
While thyme just giggled, "I'll add zest,
With fragrant whispers, I'm the best!"

A chive stood tall, with scoffs of pride,
"Just wait and see, I'll be your guide!"
The pot became a funny place,
With veggies planning a wild race.

In this oasis, all was bright,
Edible dreams took flight at night.
They laughed and danced, pure culinary glee,
In pots of clay, wild they could be!

Sunlight and Shadows

Underneath the garden's sun,
Plants had gathered, all in fun.
"With sunlight bright, we'll have a blast,"
Said one little sprout, not last!

A shadow whispered, "Don't get too bold,"
"In the shade, our stories unfold!"
Everyone giggled, playing their part,
In light or dark, it's all just art!

The daisies danced in sunlit beams,
While violets twirled in shadowed dreams.
Each petal sparkled, laughter grew,
With silly tales of what they'll do.

In sunlight's glow and shadows cast,
The garden thrived, a playful blast.
They flourished with glee, under skies so wide,
In every corner, pure joy to abide!

Blooming Within Boundaries

In a pot, I do my dance,
Roots are snug, but give me a chance.
Stretch my leaves, then laugh and sway,
Who knew here, I'd find my way?

Tiny tub, don't underestimate,
Had a dream, now I cultivate.
Sunshine smiles, watering can,
Life's a party, I take a stand!

Look at me, I'm sprouting high,
In this mug, I will comply.
Sing with bees, wave to the sun,
A pot of joy, oh what fun!

With each flower, I claim my zone,
In small confines, I'm never alone.
Watch me thrive, just take a peek,
Boundaries are for those who're weak!

The Art of Container Growth

Painting pots, a colorful spree,
A canvas for all I wish to be.
A dash of soil, a sprinkle of cheer,
Tiny worlds, just bringing near!

Stuck in a pot, my dreams take flight,
With every leaf, I hold on tight.
I jiggle and wiggle, dance a bit,
In my little realm, I just won't quit!

Water my hopes, let laughter flow,
Taking over, in case you don't know.
Seeds of humor, roots of glee,
In this quirky pot, I'm truly free!

Poised for greatness in my small space,
Growing big with a smiling face.
Watch me thrive, watch me play,
In my little pot, I find my way!

Earth's Embrace

Hugged by soil, oh what a tease,
In my pot, I swayed with ease.
Talk to worms, they're quite the crowd,
In this place, I feel so proud!

With every raindrop, a joyous cheer,
Earth's embrace, I hold it dear.
Under the sun, I joke and prance,
In this earthy bowl, I take my stance!

Neighbors are leaves, sharing the light,
In our little pot, we grow so bright.
A community of laughter, roots entwined,
In this cosmic garden, I'm well-defined!

Silly petals, voicing my glee,
In this embrace, I'm wild and free.
Each day's a giggle, each night's a hug,
With a wink from earth, it's a cozy rug!

Tiny Spaces

In tiny spaces, I find my joy,
A little corner, a tiny toy.
Dance in place, I'm never bored,
Just me and dreams, growing toward!

A ceramic castle, my royal throne,
In this small world, there's love overgrown.
Poking my leaves, peeking about,
Finding smiles without a doubt!

Each sprout a laugh, each root a cheer,
In these small realms, I persevere.
Blossom bright in this crowded bed,
What's a little pot? Just a little spread!

Thriving small but dreaming wide,
In tiny spaces, I won't hide.
With every bloom, my spirit's free,
In this little pot, just me and glee!

Mighty Journeys

In a pot, my heart takes flight,
Mighty journeys, day and night.
With every sprout, a tale to weave,
Chasing dreams, I won't believe!

Tiny seed, oh how you might,
Travel far, to reach new heights.
Under the stars, I'll wave and sing,
In a pot, I'm the blooming king!

Adventure calls, and so I sprout,
A brave little soul with no doubt.
With roots held tight, I sway and sway,
In this pot, I'm here to play!

Journey on in every petal,
With joy and laughter, who could meddle?
Mighty travels in a little space,
In the world of plants, I've found my place!

Turning Over a New Leaf

In the corner, a plant sings,
Where dust bunnies could have wings.
Watering can spills its tales,
Of green dreams riding on the gales.

Fertilizer, a party in a sack,
With worms debating, 'Shall we snack?'
Each leaf a wish, a quirky shout,
'We're alive! Don't toss us out!'

Sunlight giggles through the pane,
As pot friends play a silly game.
Shadows dance, a leafy feat,
In this crazy, green retreat.

Echoes of Enchantment

In the nursery, plants gossip loud,
Their stories wrap around the crowd.
A cactus shares a prickly joke,
While violets tease the sleepy oak.

The gardener grins, a sneaky sort,
Plotting mischief in his court.
Setting free a playful vine,
'Let's swing and sway! This garden's fine!'

A sprout claims it's the best dancer,
While herbs plot their own chancer.
Among the pots, laughter flows,
Who knows which plant really grows?

Dreams in Terra Cotta

In terracotta, dreams take flight,
Each plant whispers through the night.
With roots that tickle soil below,
And petals giggling in a show.

The pot wobbles, 'Hold me tight!'
As seedlings twirl with sheer delight.
A fern declares, 'I'm quite the star!'
While daisies argue who's bizarre.

Earthworms compete in a dirt race,
Racing roots, a slippery chase.
In this vessel, laughter blooms,
In pots where joy dispels all glooms.

Rooted Reflections

Roots entwined like best of friends,
Sharing secrets that life lends.
In leafy towers, they conspire,
Plotting giggles, never tire.

A thyme plant says, 'I'm feeling sage!'
While daisies play on a green stage.
The compost heap hums a tune,
As sunflowers flirt with the moon.

In this garden of jesting green,
Every pot holds a silly scene.
Rooted in laughter, what a find,
A funny dance of plant and mind.

Cradles of Green

In little pots, they wiggle and giggle,
Tiny sprouts in a dance, do a little jiggle.
A carrot dreams of being quite tall,
While radishes laugh, saying, 'We've got it all!'

A cactus claims it can hug, just for fun,
'I've got spikes, but I'll make you run!'
The herbs whisper secrets of flavors untold,
While peas pop out, acting oh-so-bold.

On sunny days, they bask in their fame,
Pansies pose, playing a blooming game.
In a cozy patch, there's always delight,
With every emerging sprout, pure silliness in sight.

So here's to the green, in pots and in dreams,
Where every little leaf has its own quirky schemes.
They share jokes and laugh in the garden so bright,
In the world of the wee, everything feels just right.

Cultivated Dreams

With seeds in hand, we plant with glee,
Hoping for veggies to come, just wait and see!
A tomato grins, says it's ripe for the picking,
While lettuce preens, with crisp leaves a-kicking.

Chili peppers pretend they're the spice of the year,
Making faces, heating up with no fear.
But broccoli sits with a thoughtful frown,
Wishing to grow into a crown!

Flowers parade in colors so bold,
Marigolds strut while stories unfold.
In the soil, dreams and laughter collide,
What joys await from the seeds we decide!

In pots of whims, where laughter's the sun,
Each plant a character, having such fun.
Cultivated joy in a world so serene,
Laughing at life, like a comedy scene.

Boundless Horizons in Small Vessels

In cups and cans, horizons expand,
Where daisies dream of a vast, golden land.
A sunflower stretches, but watch out, says 'Whoa!'
While thyme spins tales of how far it can grow.

Basil wants to go sailing on a breeze,
While mint insists on a party with cheese.
In every corner, a whisper ignites,
The joyous adventures of leaf-laden flights.

The kale sings songs of kaleidoscope dreams,
And the cheerfully radishes plan wild schemes.
In tiny spaces, there's magic to find,
Tiny wonders, fully intertwined.

From little pots, the stories arise,
Each plant a player in a grand enterprise.
Boundless in spirit, even in small,
These vessels hold laughter and joy for us all!

Flourishing Against the Grain

In a world of tin pans, things start to sprout,
As veggies shout, 'What's this fuss all about?'
A dandelion dreams of grandeur and pride,
While thyme plays it cool, full of zest from inside.

'Grow where you're planted!' yells a bold bean,
— A rebel at heart, like a garden queen.
But the sage with a smirk says, 'Just take a chance!'
And a row of chives joins in with a dance.

With humor in soil, and roots underground,
No boundaries here, just fun to be found.
Each sprout a comedian, cracking a grin,
In a garden of laughter, let the joy begin.

So sing with the greens, let your spirit run wild,
For life like a garden can be quite beguiled.
Against all odds, they flourish and play,
In a world full of whimsy, come join the ballet!

Petals of Promise

In tiny pots, dreams take root,
A plant's ambition, oh what a hoot!
With watering cans, we dance and sway,
Hoping green thumbs will save the day.

The daisies giggle, the roses wink,
As gardeners plot with a glass of drink.
In this wild jungle of garden glee,
Who knew plants had such quirks, you see?

Seeds whisper secrets, plan their attack,
Making their way through dirt, no lack.
With shoes on their roots and sun on their leaves,
They grow taller than tales the wise folk weave.

So let's cheer for these green little wonders,
Who bloom with laughter and joyous blunders.
With squirrels and birds performing a play,
Nature's silly antics brighten our day.

Resilient into Bloom

A speck of dirt and a bit of rain,
Who knew that such could stand the strain?
A sprout pushes up with all its might,
"Take that!" it shouts, "I'm taking flight!"

Through whirling winds and sudden frost,
These little fighters never feel lost.
With quirky faces, they stay in the game,
Resilient beings, never feeling shame.

They stretch for the sun, do a little jig,
In moments of joy, they dance so big.
Each moment counts in their leafy parade,
Oh, the frolic and fun that they'd displayed!

So next time you see a flower so bold,
Remember the tales of the bright and the gold.
That blooms with a laugh in every resound,
A triumph of laughter is cleverly found.

Nature's Quiet Canvas

In pots of clay, a world grows slow,
With strokes of green from below.
A canvas of soil where laughs emerge,
Mixed with the colors of earth's own urge.

Each petal tells tales of whimsy and cheer,
As garden gnomes smile and endear.
Sunshine splashes on like a painter's brush,
Who knew plants could have such a crush?

In hues of lavender and vibrant blue,
They chat with the bees, as friends do.
The scene is set, the stage is grand,
With nature's laughter at every hand.

Every leaf a note in life's funny song,
A reminder that here is where we belong.
So step right in and enjoy the view,
For laughter grows wild in every hue.

The Heart of the Planter

With shovel in hand and dirt on the face,
I dig with a smile, it's my special place.
Each plant a promise, each seed a dream,
Gardening's magic, or so it would seem.

A trowel's a wand in this green-fingered life,
On weekends it banishes all of my strife.
My heart grows warm with each sprouting bud,
As colors awaken from the depths of mud.

The herbs whisper jokes as the carrots play pranks,
With tomatoes blushing, they hold all the ranks.
My patio's party grows louder each day,
A friendly community in its own quirky way.

So let laughter ring out with every bloom,
In this tiny garden, I make ample room.
For joy and for silliness plant their own seed,
Turning the soil to a haven indeed.

Beginnings in Bloom

In a pot where dreams reside,
Tiny seeds begin their ride.
One thinks it's just a simple sprout,
But wait till they begin to shout!

A sunflower with a cheeky grin,
Says, "Watch me grow, let's begin!"
While daisies prance, looking quite neat,
Telling everyone, "We can't be beat!"

The soil giggles, worms do dance,
As little roots begin their prance.
It's like a party, under the sun,
With whispers of growth, oh what fun!

So here's to the future, bright and bold,
In pots of laughter, stories unfold.
Each bloom a joke, each leaf a sigh,
In the garden's midst, we all can fly!

The Language of Leaves

Leaves chatter softly, 'What's the plan?'
'Let's throw a fête, you bring the fan!'
One leaf sways, 'I'll be the star!'
While others debate just how far.

A fern claims, 'I can do a twist.'
The daisies sigh, 'Oh, don't be missed!'
'Let's take a vote!' calls out a thyme,
With petals fluttering, all in rhyme.

A worm winks, 'I'll DJ tonight!'
Making beats from left and right.
The roots all groove beneath the ground,
While petals flutter with joy unbound.

In this leafy bar, every tip's a joke,
From seedlings laughing, no one's broke.
So raise a leaf, let spirits soar,
In the garden's heart, there's always more!

Seasons of Transformation

Springtime giggles, buds anew,
'What's this? A bloom? A morning dew?'
Flowers whisper, 'We're on a spree!'
While the grass grins, 'Join the glee!'

Summer flips on its sun-kissed hat,
While plants put on their shades—how 'bout that?
Tomatoes boast, 'We're ripe and round!'
With every sip of sun, joy is found.

Come fall, the leaves put on a show,
Dancing down in a vibrant glow.
'Look at us, we're all so cool!'
While pumpkins say, 'We rule this school!'

Winter whispers, 'Time to rest,
Keep cozy dreams, we've done our best.'
In every pot, tales spin and twine,
Transforming every leaf—divine!

Echoes of the Soil

The earth chuckles, 'Here's my plan,'
Roots like fingers, they hold your hand.
'Dig deep, my friends, let's make a mess,'
With spirits high, there's no need to stress.

A beet grins, 'I'm crabby, it's true!'
And carrots laugh, 'Join the crew!'
A daffodil shouts, 'I've got the flair,'
While a mossy patch croons with care.

Squirrels hop, with acorns in tow,
They share the secrets the soil knows.
Every bug has a trick or two,
In this pot of stories, laughter's the glue.

So here's to the dirt, to laughter's might,
Growing together, what a delight!
With each seed sown, and every cheer,
Echoes of joy, in every tier.

Saplings of Change

In a jar I found a sprout,
It shouted, "Let me out!"
A wiggle here, a wiggle there,
I laughed at roots with such wild flair.

This tiny thyme has dreams so grand,
It wants to travel, see the land.
But stuck in soil, it can't take flight,
A sassy plant, oh what a sight!

Gone is the sage, who made the stew,
In its place, a cactus grew.
With prickly thoughts, it wants to share,
A recipe for a prickly pear.

The basil danced, oh what a tease,
It spun around with perfect ease.
Homemade pesto it swears to make,
From these green dreams, our taste buds quake!

Earthbound Visions

A sunflower with a playful grin,
Declared, "I'm ready to begin!"
I said, "But dear, you're stuck right here!"
It shrugged, "I'll bloom, have no fear!"

The daisies laughed, they knew the trick,
They twirled and spun—oh how they flick!
With petals bright and cheer so spry,
They winked at worms that drifted by.

A pot of dirt, a stroke of fate,
The parsley claimed to be first-rate.
But when it saw the rosemary,
It sighed, "Why can't we fly and be free?"

An amaryllis wore a crown,
Declared it would never, ever frown.
But inside soil, it sat and reigned,
In the kingdom of the slightly constrained.

Whispers of Growth

A seed once dreamed of being tall,
But ended up just taking calls.
It sighs while soaking sunlit rays,
"Is this my life?" it often weighs.

The mint lets out a cheeky laugh,
"Just gives me time, I'll find my path!"
In smoothies, teas, or pies so sweet,
It's curious how it finds its beat.

The fern is wise, but quite aloof,
It often questions the angle of its roof.
"Is being green the height of flair?"
It pondered deep while losing hair.

From every nook, new tales unfurl,
Of herbs that dance and roots that twirl.
In every pot, a story spins,
Of leafy dreams, where laughter begins.

Vessel of Wishes

In a fancy pot, a wish took root,
It dreamed of shoes, a snazzy suit.
But as a peony, it realized,
Fashion week is not where it resides.

A sage so smart, it gave advice,
"Just stay, enjoy this pot. It's nice!"
But the sage once yearned for a big parade,
Now it's stuck in a flower trade.

An anxious orchid thought it knew,
"I'll blossom bright to steal the view!"
But in this vessel, it learned the score,
Beauty's tricky, who could ask for more?

And every pot's a tiny dream,
Where aspirations shimmy and gleam.
With every leaf, our hopes take flight,
In this garden of giggles, all feels right.

Nature's Quiet Promises

A little seed sat with a grin,
It thought of all the fun within.
"I'll sprout and dance, I swear I will,
Just need some sun, some rain, and thrill!"

The worms were planning, quite the show,
They wore tiny hats and stole the glow.
"Let's throw a party in this pot,
And see who can grow the funniest plot!"

The raindrops laughed as they fell down,
Their splashes made a bubbly crown.
"I'm here to help with all your aims,
Let's grow together, play some games!"

So under leaves, they shared a cheer,
Each sprout a dream, each root a peer.
With giggles mixed in soil and clay,
A garden's laugh brightened the day.

Blossoms Beyond the Boundaries

Across the fence, the flowers peep,
They dream of worlds where petals leap.
"Let's break the rules, let's be bold,
And see what secrets we can hold!"

The daisies donned their wildest dress,
With polka dots, they felt no stress.
"I'll teach you how to sway and spin,
Just watch out for the bee with a grin!"

The sun chuckled, a friendly tease,
As shadows danced upon the leaves.
"Our borders? Just a silly myth,
Let's explore beyond, it's time to skit!"

With laughter bright in every hue,
They gathered dreams like morning dew.
In every bloom, a story laid,
Of silly wishes both made and played.

Embracing Earth

Down in the dirt, they throw a bash,
With muddy boots and a happy splash.
"Let's hug the ground, give roots a cheer,
With tickles and laughter, we'll draw near!"

The worms are wigglers, stars of the show,
In the soil dance, they steal the glow.
"Slide over here, let's twirl and roll,
Feel the earth giggle from deep in its soul!"

"Have you heard the tale of the daffodil,
Who danced so much it gave a thrill?
She leaped so high, she tripped and spun,
Fell into a pot, and that's how it's done!"

So here we sit, in dirt galore,
Creating chaos, forevermore.
With winks and whispers shared so sweet,
We're planting joy where roots now meet.

Fertile Fantasies

Tiny dreams root deep in the ground,
Dancing with visions that swirl around.
"What if we grew a tree made of cheese?
Or flowers that giggle, so silly, so frees!"

The garden gnomes heard a quite funny tale,
Of a carrot that hosted a bright, grand sale.
"Come buy a smile, or perhaps a frown,
Hurry, before the rainbow turns brown!"

With every sprout, a new thought appeared,
Of whimsical worlds that drew us near.
"Let's plant bubblegum or chocolate trees,
And share our laughter in the evening breeze!"

So with a wink, they took their chance,
In fields of dreams, they'd surely dance.
With every laugh, a seed would sprout,
In a world where dreams can twist and shout.

Flourishing Fragments

In a pot sits a sprout, quite small,
Thinking it's destined to rule them all.
Leaves waving like it's got some flair,
But really just hopes for a little fresh air.

A cactus dreams of being a rose,
With spiky ambitions that nobody knows.
It poses as if it's got style to lend,
While leaving a prick for each hapless friend.

The herbs chat loudly, gossip on the side,
As basil brags of its culinary pride.
Thyme rolls its eyes at such silly talk,
While mint sneaks away for a nonchalant walk.

When the sun shines bright, they throw a parade,
Each little leaf in an anarchist braid.
Together they flourish, unlike any yard,
Creating a circus that you can't disregard.

Potting the Unseen

Once there was a seed who longed to sprout,
But feared the dirt would make it pout.
'What if I grow, and I'm just a weed?'
The seed pondered deep; oh, the things it would need!

A worm popped up, with a grin quite sly,
'Just trust me, dear seed, and give it a try!'
So the seed took the plunge, in soil it did dive,
Dreaming of being a plant that's alive.

It stretched for the sun like it was its kin,
But tangled in weeds, oh where to begin?
'Is this my life, in a tangle of strife?
Or will I bloom, and dance with delight?'

But the tale twisted; it grew so spry,
Breaking free from the weeds with a laugh in the sky.
'Look at me now!' it yelled with glee,
Turning the odds into pure jubilee!

Manifesting Moments

A sunflower dreamed of pop star fame,
With its petals like glitter, it played a big game.
It staged an audition with wild little twirls,
But all it attracted were a bunch of squirrels.

The beans were jealous, growing lean and tall,
As they whispered together, 'Who's the fairest of all?'
Yet during lunch breaks, when no one would care,
They'd slip into shadows for a secret affair.

A tomato laughed, with its juicy delight,
While plotting to conquer the salad tonight.
It practiced its roll, and with a fierce shout,
It declared, 'Who needs dressing, let's leave those out!'

Through sunlight and raindrops, they danced in their pots,

Turning every mishap into glittering plots.
In this garden of giggles, with joy that abounds,
Every petal and leaf wrote their own silly sounds.

Imprints in the Earth

In a corner of the yard, where chaos would reign,
Lies a collection of herbs far too proud to complain.
They swap their secrets with roots intertwined,
Creating a tale that's humorously blind.

The sage is wise, or so it insists,
'But let's not forget about my garlic twist!'
With antics and accents, they banter all day,
Creating a sitcom in their own little way.

A rogue weed declares, 'I'm part of the game!'
With a wild little wink, 'You'll remember my name!'
But the flowers just giggle, little heads held high,
'You'll never fit in, you awkward old guy!'

Yet as seasons shift, and they all grow old,
They realize the laughter is the treasure they hold.
So in every sprout, an imprint will stay,
A patch of pure joy that won't fade away.

Soil-Sung Adventures

In a pot on the sill, a dream resides,
Whispers of soil where ambition abides.
A sprout with a grin, reaches for the light,
Saying, "Watch out world, I'm ready to bite!"

Beans making jokes, while carrots just stare,
Roots tangled in laughter, without a care.
Tomatoes in shades, pink and red too,
Claiming, "We're ripe, and we're ready for stew!"

Bees buzzing in tune, a dance in the air,
Pollination's the game, a sweet love affair.
Every little leaf has a quirk of its own,
In this pot full of giggles, no seed feels alone!

So come take a peek at this green leafy fest,
Where every plant thinks it's truly the best.
Life's a funny sketch in this garden we know,
Dig deep in the soil, let your laughter grow!

Nurtured by Sunbeams

Tiny sprouts stretch, yawning at dawn,
Grabbing rays of sunshine before they're all gone.
A dwarf sunflower giggles, "Look at me shine!"
While the parsley snickers, "I'm tasting divine!"

Cucumber dreams of pickles in jars,
Chasing fireflies and counting the stars.
Radishes dress up, in colors so bold,
"Fashion week? We're ready! Watch our roots unfold!"

An oregano lad says, "I'm quite the spice!"
"I could make salads taste so very nice."
Peppers boast heat to tickle your tongue,
While marigolds dance, their praises well sung!

So under the sunbeams, we flourish and play,
In this garden's embrace, let worries drift away.
With each cheerful bloom, the world seems just fine,
Nurtured by laughter, in this life's garden shrine!

Growth in Every Corner

A little pot here, a seed placed with care,
Sprouting up laughter, floating in air.
There's rocket in bloom with a bold, zesty flair,
While a timid pea pod whispers, "Life's fair!"

We've got basil that dreams, glimmering with zest,
Imitating herbs that think they're the best.
Thyme chimes in, "Don't forget about me!
I bring flavor galore, can't you see?"

Lettuce feuds with weeds, a comical clash,
"Out of my way!" says the kale in a flash.
Spinach packs muscles, flexing roots proud,
"I'm here to bulk up, I'll stand out in a crowd!"

In every little corner, a story unfolds,
With plants full of humor, and jokes never old.
So join in the fun, let your spirits soar,
In this garden of quirks, there's always more!

Hidden Gardens of Potential

Behind the fence, oh what a sight,
Secrets unravel, in morning's light.
A broccoli kingdom, ruled by the sprout,
Proclaiming, "All praise, I'm here to hold out!"

The thyme team whispers plots full of fun,
"Let's start a rally, we'll soon be number one!"
Celery minions dance, in long green lines,
While radishes plan pranks, forming secret designs.

Lettuce and chard fight over the sun,
Their leafy debates are an absolute run.
"High five!" say the herbs, sticking together,
In their leafy world, it's all light as a feather!

So take a step back and soak in the cheer,
These hidden gardens bring joy, that's clear.
Where every petal and leaf tells a jest,
Embracing our dreams, a green-fingered quest!

www.ingramcontent.com/pod-product-compliance
Lightning Source LLC
Chambersburg PA
CBHW070309120526
44590CB00017B/2606